101 MATH JOKES

Erin O'Connor and Chrissy Bozik

illustrations by Bill Dickson

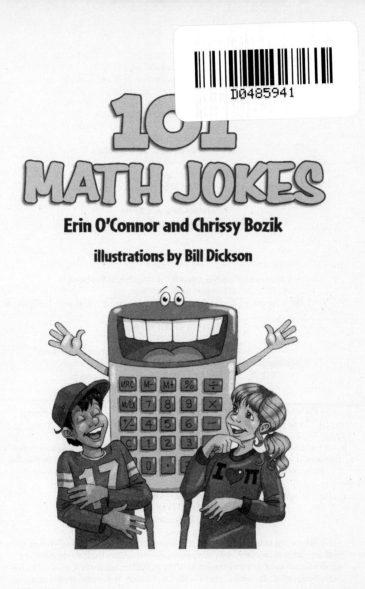

Scholastic Canada Ltd.

Toronto New York London Auckland Sydney
Mexico City New Delhi Hong Kong Buenos Aires

Scholastic Canada Ltd.
604 King Street West, Toronto, Ontario M5V 1E1, Canada

Scholastic Inc.
557 Broadway, New York, NY 10012, USA

Scholastic Australia Pty Limited
PO Box 579, Gosford, NSW 2250, Australia

Scholastic New Zealand Limited
Private Bag 94407, Botany, Manukau 2163, New Zealand

Scholastic Children's Books
Euston House, 24 Eversholt Street, London NW1 1DB, UK

Library and Archives Canada Cataloguing in Publication
O'Connor, Erin, 1968 Sept. 21-
101 math jokes / Erin O'Connor and Chrissy Bozik ; illustrator, Bill Dickson.

ISBN 978-1-4431-0738-9

1. Canadian wit and humor (English)--Juvenile literature.
2. Mathematics--Juvenile humor. I. Bozik, Chrissy II. Dickson, Bill
III. Title. IV. Title: One hundred and one math jokes.
V. Title: One hundred one math jokes.

PS8375.O2685 2011   jC817.008'036   C2010-907345-2

6 5 4 3 2 1   Printed in Canada 121   11 12 13 14 15

We're Number Fun

What's the hungriest number?

Seven — because seven eight nine!

Why did −5 always frown?

Because he was a negative number.

Why did the boy eat a bowl of numbers for breakfast?

They're grrreight!

Why was 15 always so confident?

She was a positive number.

Why did I, V and X keep wandering off?

Because they're Roman numerals!

Why does a number line make such a good friend?

Because you can always count on it!

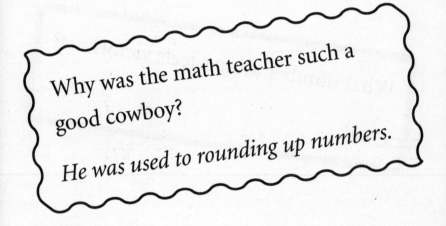

Why was the math teacher such a good cowboy?

He was used to rounding up numbers.

What number always feels victorious?

One!

What did the numbers do at the hoedown?

A line dance!

What instrument does 6 − 4 play?

The two*ba!*

Why did 3, 5 and 7 put socks on their heads and hop around singing "Happy Birthday"?

Because they were odd numbers!

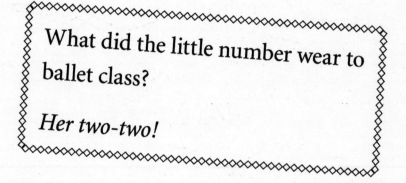

What did the little number wear to ballet class?

Her two-two!

What kind of fort did the numbers build?

*A three*house*!*

How does 1 × 1 get ready for dinner?

It sets the times table!

Get in Shape

Why did the shapes disappear?

Because they were polygons.

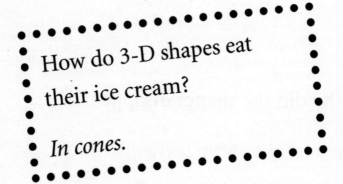

How do 3-D shapes eat their ice cream?

In cones.

Why weren't the cube and the cone afraid of the monster?

Because they had no sphere!

What do circles eat at Thanksgiving?

Pumpkin pi!

Why did the cube wear so much makeup?

Because she had 6 faces!

What did the 10-sided figure say
when a flood washed away his porch?

Decagon!

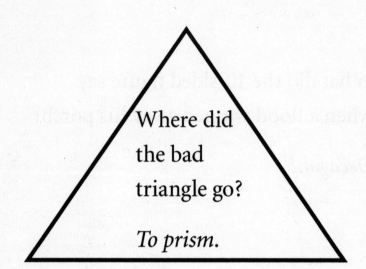

Where did
the bad
triangle go?

To prism.

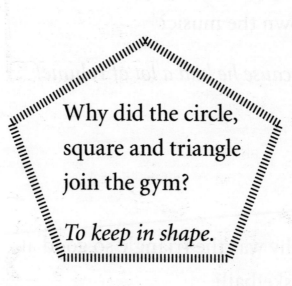

Why did the circle, square and triangle join the gym?

To keep in shape.

Why did the big cylinder have to turn down the music?

Because he had a lot of volume!

Why was the triangle so good at basketball?

He could always make a three-pointer.

What do country-and-western shapes do at the prom?

Square dance!

How did King Arthur
reward the brave circle?

He dubbed him Sir
Cumference.

What kind of triangle loves to skate?

An iceoceles triangle!

What does a circle do when it loses something?

It looks round.

FRACTION ACTION

Why didn't 4 call 9?

He didn't half her number.

What does a mommy graph make for dessert?

A pie chart!

What did the denominator say to her best friend, the numerator?

You're tops!

Why did 8/5 get sent to the principal's office?

Because he'd been an improper fraction!

Why did the decimal win the debate?

Because he made a good point.

Why didn't anybody like the average number?

Because she was mean!

Why didn't the fraction pass his math test?

He only did half the work!

Why was 5.5 late for 3.2's birthday party?

He couldn't find the right decimal place.

What king loved fractions?

Henry the Eighth.

Why couldn't 2/10 relax?

He was two tenths!

Measuring **Up**

How did the little hand always know which way to turn?

Because he was clockwise.

Who is the king of measurement?

The ruler!

Where did the scale buy a puppy?

At the pound!

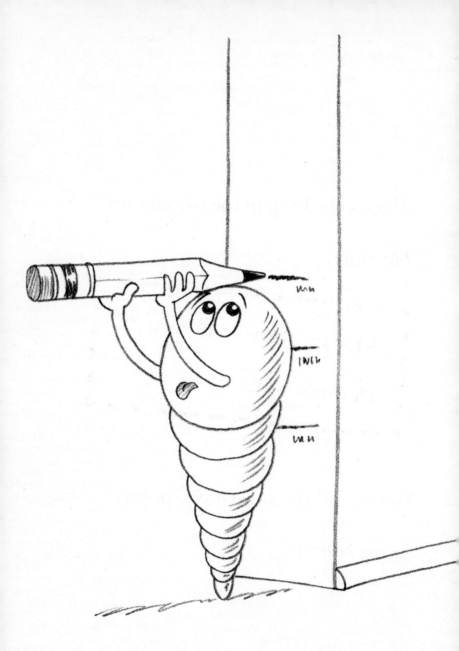

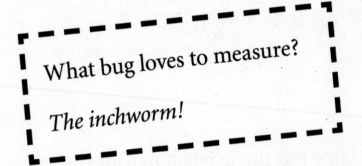

What bug loves to measure?

The inchworm!

Why is a dollar so smart?

Because it has lots of cents!

How did the jellyfish pay for his lunch?

With a sand dollar!

When does 1 come *after* 12?

When it's on a clock!

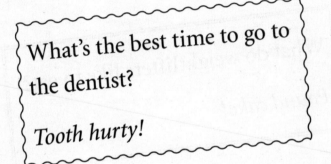

What's the best time to go to the dentist?

Tooth hurty!

What do weightlifters like to eat?

Pound cake!

What time is it when the quarter chases the loonie?

A quarter after one!

How do weights send important messages?

By telegram!

GEOMETRY COMEDY

Why did Acute move next door to Obtuse?

Because they wanted to be adjacent angles.

How does an angle plow his field?

With a pro-tractor!

Why did the girl angle have a crush on the boy angle?

Because he was acute.

Why did the 90-degree angle win the argument?

Because she was right!

How did X and Y cut down the tree?

With their axis!

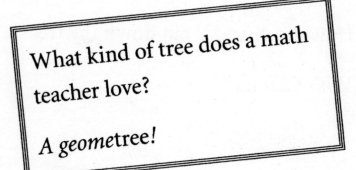

What kind of tree does a math teacher love?

A geometree!

Why did the 60-degree angle say he liked the 30-degree angle's outfit?

Because he was a complimentary *angle!*

Why couldn't the square go straight home?

It lived around the corner.

Math Class
LOL

How do math teachers dry their clothes?

On a number line.

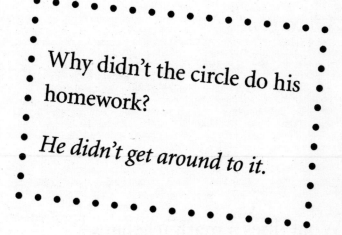

Why didn't the circle do his homework?

He didn't get around to it.

What did the witch curse the math teacher with?

A hexagon!

What does a math teacher's parrot say?

Polygon want a cracker!

Why didn't the equation like track and field?

Because he wasn't a very good mathlete!

Why did the math teacher go to the guidance counsellor?

He had number problems.

Why did the math teacher need a comb?

Because her hair was full of rectangles.

What math tool points north?

A compass!

How do polygons get to school?

On a rhombus!

Why did the student stand with his back to the class?

Because the teacher asked him to count backwards!

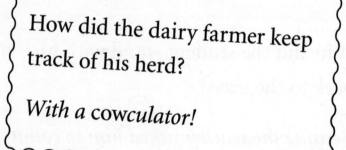

How did the dairy farmer keep track of his herd?

With a cowculator!

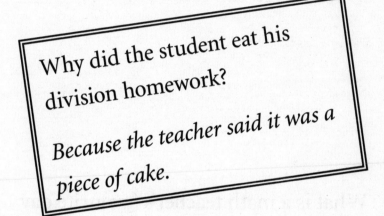

Why did the student eat his division homework?

Because the teacher said it was a piece of cake.

What do you get when you cross a person with a calculator?

Someone you can count on.

What is a math teacher's favourite day of the week?

Twos*day!*

Why did the student stand outside of the second-grade classroom to count?

Because the teacher told him to count by twos!

Let's Have Sum Fun

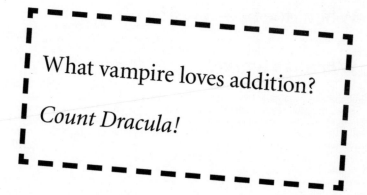

What vampire loves addition?

Count Dracula!

Why didn't 1 and 2 hang out?

Because 3's a crowd.

When does 2 + 3 = 4?

When it's wrong!

What sport do 9 and 1 like to play?

Tennis!

What is addition's favourite season?

Summer!

Knock knock.
Who's there?
3 + 3 =
3 + 3 = who?
No, 3 + 3 = 6!

What is 1 fish + 1 fish?

*A two*na *fish!*

Why is a kitchen good at
adding things?

It has a counter!

What's 6 + 1's favourite soft drink?

7UP!

What did 2 and 2 order at the Chinese restaurant?

Four*tune cookies!*

Why did the judge find 1 + 1 = 3 guilty?

Because her evidence didn't add up!

Why is addition so heavy?

Because you have to carry all the numbers!

If you have 15 marbles and you lose 8 marbles, what do you have?

Problems!

What kind of gum does 2 like?

Dubble Bubble.

If you have $33 and your grandma gives you $78, what do you have?

A very nice grandma!

What kind of juice does 4 + 1 like?

Five Alive!

How do 1 and 2 celebrate Christmas?

They decorate a three!

Ph.D.

Why couldn't trigonometry get a loan?

Because no one would cosine!

Why was the word problem such a good dancer?

*Because she had algo*rhythm.

Why was the baby math problem crying?

Because she needed formula.

What happened when 8 lay down?

He felt infinitely better!

What happened to the tree that was good at math?

It got square roots.

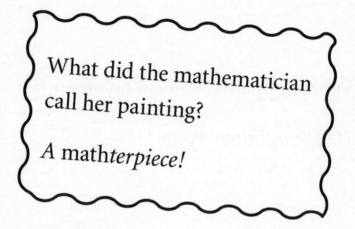

What did the mathematician call her painting?

*A math*terpiece!

Why did the polygon fail the driving test?

He couldn't parallelogram park.

What kind of pop did 9 offer 3?

Square-root beer.

Why was the ordered pair so fashionable?

Because she was good with coordinates.

What is a math teacher's favourite type of music?

Algorithm and blues!

What kind of math does plankton love?

Algaebra!

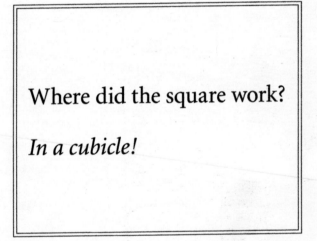

Where did the square work?

In a cubicle!